HOGWASH!™

Written by Charlie Heath

Cover Art: Tommy Orrico
Illustrated by Kathleen Russell, Tommy Orrico & Charlie Heath

Published by
Walrus Productions
Seattle

Published by Walrus Productions
4805 N.E. 106th Street, Seattle WA 98125

Telephone (206) 364-4365 Fax (206) 362-2834
web site: www.walrusproductions.com

Written by Charlie Heath
Illustrated by Kathleen Russell, Tommy Orrico & Charlie Heath

Layout and typography by Larry Wall / Urbanphotolab
Edited by Margie Norman
Printed by Vaughan Printing, Nashville, Tennessee

Library of Congress Catalog Number 2001-126910

Heath, Charlie.
    HOGWASH! / Charlie Heath

ISBN 1-892851-00-8
1. Pigs--Humor. 2.Pigs--Humor, Pictorial. I. Title

Printed in the United States of America

10 9 8 7 6 5 4 3 2 1

Dedicated to:

My wife Carilyn and my sister Julia
And the memory of our parents

Especially dedicated to

My Grandfather and Namesake
Charlie, Traffic Manager of The Rath Packing Company
who of himself said, " I tell the pigs where to go."

Why can't pigs keep secrets?

Because they're born squealers

What are the three sizes of pig?

Pig

Pigger

Piggest

What do pigs like to do
on a nice summer day?

What day is it when a pig visits the butcher?

GROUND HOG DAY!

Pigs don't like shopping downtown
because there is ...

Why won't pigs talk about pigs?

They hate to Talk Chop!

What was the real origin
of the universe?

The Pig Bang Theory

Should a pig answer the door?

only if OPPORKTUNITY knocks

"High on the Hog"

Have you ever seen a pig
with 3 eyes?

Why do pigs drink coffee?

For a little Pig-Me-Up

Pigs know they got it made
when ...

they finally make it
to the Pig Leagues!

A pig doing well is ...

A HAM ON A ROLL!

Where do pigs like
going on vacation?

The Tropigs

Where do pigs march?

In the Swiners Day Parade

What do pigs need to travel abroad?

Good Day!

... to a French pig.

Will pigs ever smell sweet?

What do Mother Pigs say?

"Don't pig your nose!"

What do old sows wear?

Suppork hose

How do lowly pigs feel?

Inpignificant

Where do pigs go to college?

What do you call pigs
that go trick or treating?

HALLOWIENERS!

Who is a famous pig painter?

Pigasso

What language do pigs speak?

What do pigs practice?

The hamly art
of self-offense

What kind of stories do pigs tell?

Pig Tales

What do you call a pig that tells the same story over and over?

A Boar

What makes pigs laugh?

Watching
stand-up comedihams
tell one-swiners

Where do pigs go when they die?

Hog Heaven!!!

How do pigs in trouble get help?

They join a suppork group!

Where do bankrupt pigs go?

Pork Belly Up

Why do pigs visit Fortune Tellers?

Where do pigs save their money?

What do pig pals enjoy?

A sense of Hamardarie!

What do pig waiters ask?

"May I show you the Swine List?"

Where do pigs go
after they get married?

On their Hogeymoon

What do you call a pig
with a hammer?

A construction porker

What are pigs good for?

Grunt Work

Who is the King of Hog & Roll?

What instrument
do pigs like to play in a band?

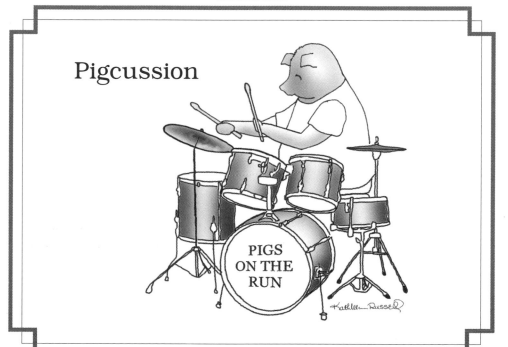

Who entertains pigs?

Pork Belly Dancers

What pigs sailed the high seas?

Pigrates

and

Baconeers

Who shows up
on pigs' family trees?

Their hamcesters

How do pigs get fat?

BY PORKING OUT!!!

What breakfast meal
does a chicken participate in
but the pig
is completely committed to?

Ham & Eggs

Where can pigs see stars?

The corner of Hoggywood & Swine

Do pigs drink?

Just a little snort now and then

Who do bad people
fear the most?

THE
PIGS!

Why did the pig get arrested?

What do pigs call
a hot dog and a beer?

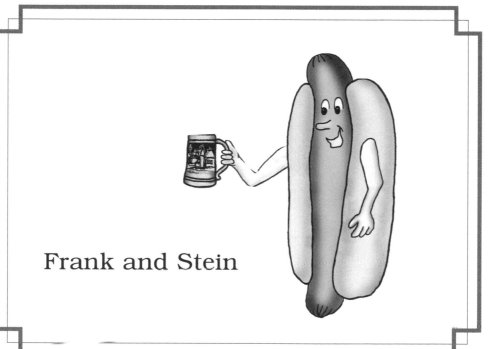

Frank and Stein

Where do you put
the piggest criminals?

Solitary Conswinement

What was the name
of a prehistoric pig?

Pigasaurus

What do Father Pigs say?

"Son, you'll be a Ham someday."

What is a pig's favorite ballet?

Swine Lake

What Shakespeare play
do pigs like the most?

HAMLET

What is a famous Greek Myth?

What do you call a pig
that does silly things
to get attention?

A Hamster

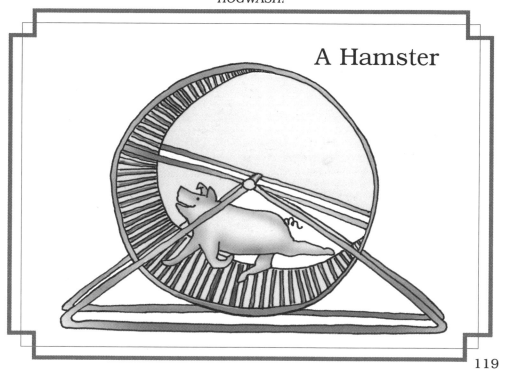

What reveals a pig's innermost thoughts?

The Oink Blot Test!

How do pigs introduce themselves?

They shake hams

Who is the unknown pig ancestor?

The missing oink

What does Grade "A" Pork
mean to a pig?

Hog Wild School District

First Hamester Kindergarten

REPORK CARD

Student- Ollie Oink

Grade

	Grade
Deporkment	A
Odorliness	A+
Pig Penmanship	A
Smelling	A

What is the
piggest city in Oregon?

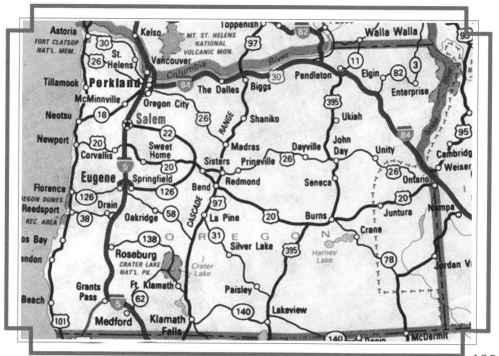

What do French pigs do
after going to the market?

They say, "Oui! Oui! Oui!"
all the way home

What do you call
a pig accountant?

A Pork and Bean Counter

To whom does a pig Valentine go?

PIGGY SUE

What kind of hog
does a pig ride?

Pork Chopper

What does a pig need
to visit a doctor?

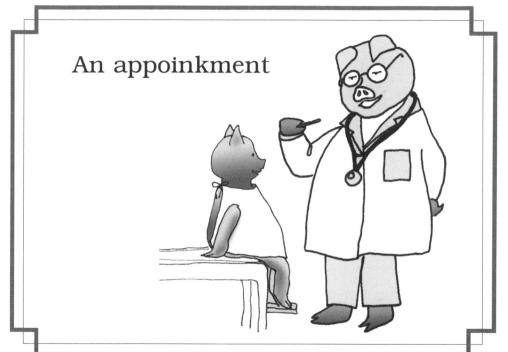

An appoinkment

How do you treat a pig owie?

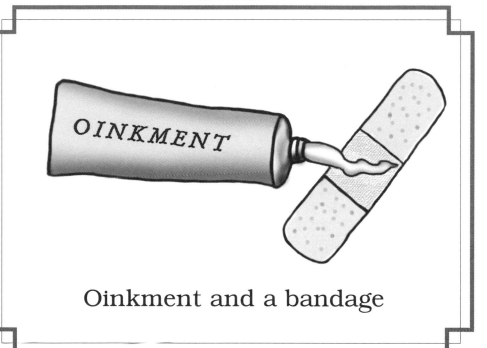

Oinkment and a bandage

How do you get to the hogspital?

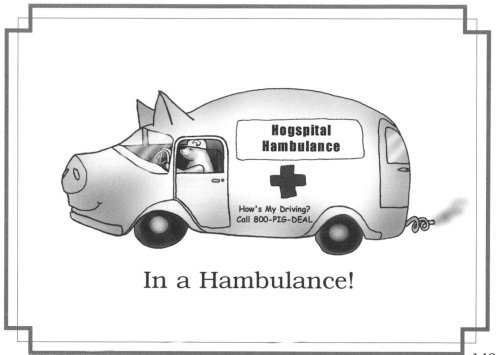

In a Hambulance!

Why do doctors care for pigs?

What do you call a pig
who takes up more than one lane?

Why be nice to pigs?

Because you shouldn't bite
the Hams that feed you!

Why do pigs get along so well?

Pigs aren't *really* lazy ...

They are just wasting swine

A Hoggerel Verse

There once was a sow named Sue
who knew not quite what to do
hated being a pig
wanted some other gig
and alas wound up in a stew.

The ***HOGWASH*** is over …

When the
Fat Sow
Has Sung!

ABOUT THE AUTHOR

Charles D. Heath (Charlie to his family, which he is asking you to join just for the fun of it, and Chuck to the rest of the world) lives with his wife, Carilyn, but no piglets, in Onalaska, Wisconsin. He is a lawyer, businessman, and riddle maker.

Hogwash! is his first book of riddles but only the first in the Hogwash! series. The second book, Hogwash! Too - The Menagerie, will show you the Hogwash! is not just about pigs. Among other riddles, you will learn the answers to "Why do elephants itch?" and "Should porpoises be punished?"

Visit our web site: www.walrusproductions.com

To contact the author:

Charlie Heath
P.O. Box 3395 LaCrosse, Wisconsin 54601-3395

Telephone (608) 796-5010
Fax (608) 796-5437

OTHER FUN BOOKS

A whimsical collection of delightful books to
make you think, chuckle, self-motivate & lift your spirits.

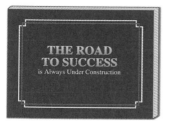

Road to Success

Motherhood

Achieve Your Dreams

Computer Byte

Garden Grow

View from Litter Box

ORDER ADDITIONAL BOOKS AS GIFTS

	qty	
HOGWASH!	qty____	@ **8.95 Each** ____
THE ROAD TO SUCCESS	qty____	@ 7.95 Each ____
ACHIEVE YOUR DREAMS	qty____	@ 7.95 Each ____
MOTHERHOOD	qty____	@ 7.95 Each ____
VIEW FROM LITTER BOX	qty____	@ 7.95 Each ____
KITTY LITTERATURE	qty____	@ 7.95 Each ____
DOGGIE TALES	qty____	@ 7.95 Each ____
GOLFING IMPAIRED	qty____	@ 7.95 Each ____
COMPUTER BYTE	qty____	@ 7.95 Each ____
GARDEN GROW	qty____	@ 7.95 Each ____

Add 2.00 for shipping for 1st book, 50¢ ea. thereafter ____

WA State residents only: add applicable sales tax
Canadian & Foreign orders: double S & H charges & pay in US Funds
Order online or by phone: MasterCard / VISA accepted

web site **www.walrusproductions.com**

Total ____

Walrus Productions
4805 N.E. 106th St
Seattle, WA 98125
(206) 364-4365

Prices subject to change

These books may be ordered through your local book store.

Name ____
Address ____
City ____
State-Zip ____